My Handsome Reflection Though

William Morton

Presentation by *BookLeaf Publishing*

Web: www.bookleafpub.com

E-mail: info@bookleafpub.com

ISBN: 9789357740296

First edition 2023

Rejected Jokes

I was kidnapped by mimes.

 They threatened to do unspeakable things to me.

 I feel it was insensitive getting my short friend a bonsai tree.

 I worked at a sad soda making facility and it was soda pressing.

I have respect for sauces, I close the door if I see ranch dressing.

 I can do sound effects which makes me an expert speaker.

I like to do things covertly which is why I wear sneakers.

Don't Hug, I Get Scared Easily

Dress for the job I want, not the job I have.
Which I took into consideration as I wear
sweatpants to work.
I want them to know I want to do my job
remote.
These jobs say to have confidence, to have
experience but what does that mean?
The choice for cushion with not much growth or
following dreams with hope.
Don't perform to others expectations and then
put a caption on it.
Don't pace yourself with hesitancy, do what you
want and if you stumble, someone is going to
conveniently catch.

Aux In My Car

The respiratory system is a reflection of
struggling with disillusionment.
The aspirations of anticipation leave me with
deflation and depression.
What I say and what I do, leave me with much
ado.
I struggle with existentialism and contemplation.
I need to accomplish or attempt to cope.
The car I drive isn't here and I need to replace
the radio.
My safety is in the sound or so I thought, now
opinionated noise is here.
The not wanted noise is now what I face.
The joy of jokes now gets replaced by hopes and
subconsciously surprises listeners.
Not getting reassurance from those sounds lets
my imagination do what it can do.
The radio is a metaphor for the discontentment.
The car is me and I feel like the road is testing
me, thought in my consciousness.
Wall in my mind breaks and now the dark
thoughts are at the front.

Stressed For The Moment

My humor is self reference, self reflecting; synonyms.
I thought I was only a performer on stage but I put on a happy face when sad.
I want to remove the theater and tech from my stage persona.
 Yet I have other things for me that make me more talented.
 I have the voice and platform when there are others that are voiceless.
Handsome, has height and educated so how can I feel discontentment?
There is so much interconnection.
The idea when from "what are your dreams?" to "what do you do?"
 Don't release hopes on dreams but performers don't get recognition in accordance to their accomplishments.

The Man That Looks At Me In My Reflection

I was taught that growing up meant getting less afraid and more manly.
I get accompanied with anxiety.
Didn't grow up to replace my fears.
My fears grew up with me.
That fear is a manifestation of my self-loathing.
Sympathizing with me.
I whiff to get back that memory.
Today society expects me to grow up.
Having an imagination doesn't get me that safe but boring job.
The constant fear of adulthood.
Wanting to get cash at the cost of mental struggles.
Representation of carefree.

Modern Day Record Player

I feel like a poser for owning a modern record
player.
The impostor phenomenon doesn't make me feel
confident.
I don't know if I should get what I get.
I do things metaphorically to advance my career.
The reliance of validation.
I jot down notes for mental health.
The stress that I can accept what I can do.
I work so consistently that I focus on my career.

Aches

The migraine that I suffered is a metaphor.
Headaches that I faced on my face doesn't
necessarily say I'm the problem.
The alarm in my mind, psyching me in my
psyche.
Conflicting thoughts, representing those
conflicting parts of me.
Hesitation to say I get depression so I say I get
depressed thoughts.
Taboo to me unless I look at my reflection.
My reflection is to me but if I don't speak, the
voiceless are affected.

Crazed Fan

Let me say what I can, hear the ramblings of a psycho man.
I get panic attacks and go on whinging.
Due to that, I don't feel as if I'm competent to talk.
The pain of conversation.
The struggle of anxiety.
I feel like I need to grasp though I feel sane.
I guess I need more meds.

Lost Childhood

The reason that going places is so enjoyed is the
release of stress it gives.
Dance for this moment.
The lethargic inertness cause from an excessive
party.
In childhood, I dreamt of acceptance.
Flaunting thoughts that get mature.
Now I look at those dreams that are deprecated.
 I lost so much hope in society.

Follow The Nose For Memories

Desperation for progression but battling constraints.
Thoughts for compliments but only get complaints.
Overstayed and so sick my thoughts are overplayed.
I saw my fears as shrinking things.
I look at a photo to revisit my memory.
That photo screams at me for cash and screams at me.
I follow my nose but get irritated that I can't recognize my thought visits.
If I recognized the aroma, my nose would get subjected to lits.

Grow To Those Expectations

Let me say with patronizing flow.
If the hard, shivering cold doesn't show.
There is corporations on the block that are
needy.
The corporations get a taste of control and get
greedy.
Those people on the sidewalk aren't characters in
your show.
Sometimes it takes the rude confrontation to let
the lion from within.
In this convoluted society, some of us need thick
skin.
Growing up entitled lets you get rude.
What are you going to do when they don't cater
to your attitude?
Fending for yourself isn't exciting.
The struggles don't stop so keep fighting.
Hey congrats on graduating.
Now keep on doing and relax with the
hesitating.

Literary Lyrics

I sense this sense, an outward occurrence.
Something I don't know from whence, but has
let me feel competently spent.
A phenomenon in such, as I say that how I feel
is me saying I don't know much.
This intelligence wordplay isn't me but yet I use
it as my wit-like crutch.
These environments and settings are part of the
problem.
I do what I can to not toot my metaphoric horn
but yet it looks like low my volume.
Fear of such failure.
Fear of such success.
I need to subdue this ruthless contest.

Who I Act Like Isn't Who I Was

Singing to myself in a sorrowful voice.
Loneliness feel with regret.
Interpret that as focusing on the past.
I need to cleanse.
Processing the thoughts that put me on this road.
I can't rewind the memories.
I need to go with sorrow.

Emo Romance

Let me introduce the characters, young man and
woman.
Heteronormative but cliche and clear.
 Rough around the edges and she loved to dance.
Her friends and her didn't like that they were
mutually interested.
High standards for significant others.
The same friends that affected her decision to
reject his style are his fans.
Substance can show character.

The Concept That Gets Applause

The concept of joy.
This customer/ dancer is a result of
interconnected stances.
Self-indulgent and hedonistic.
Living as an artist, observing culture isn't low.
 Voice that can get shared but stay content
without spectators to validate.
I want to stay honest on stage, not give a show
that wasn't my own.
I don't know what I could do if I couldn't say
things as a joke.

They Say What Needs To Get heard

The news likes to focus on corporate media and
attention hungry customers.
If they were to play songs, they would seem
have their own agendas.
These networks are advocating feminism yet use
females to conduct interviews.
Companies that sponsor news get what they
want from what they do.
Dangers from products are downplayed.
The news conveniently shows only what they
want.
Sponsors say that products are safe.

Career Path

I don't know if I feel joy.
My career path is heavily a service, I say this or
write this and they get results.
Such a career on stage that can result in mental
illness.
That joy doesn't specify.
Rhetoric in a way that provokes thought.
I hope that my jokes let others get from
problems.
I understand if my jokes are corny but I hope
there was a part that was enjoyed.
I struggle with joy, though I had my wins.
If I was to constantly get joy, I don't know if that
what I want so I get sad to get joy.

I Say Thoughts That Are Regular

I don't like when people say that I'm nice.
They say that I was educated from my
vernacular.
Yes I read books, I love to sort words with
lyrics.
That doesn't make me feel like I should on a
pedestal.
My jokes are for those that need, but the
individual in need is me.
Do not clamor to me if I do not entertain or if
my jokes aren't in that niche.
Don't look at me as a hero, look at me as part of
the joke.

Edited Reflections

I took occurrences and turned those into jokes.
Narrated regular occurrences and going to the
store in a way that has joy.
I don't know if I was honest or if I edited
honesty.
Look at what I can do.
Look at what I could do.
I don't care for honest thoughts, I rather say what
I thought I thought.
Yeah I look at me and look at my reflection,
though my thoughts edit my reflection.